Radical Sports

MOUNTAIN Biking

Kirk Bizley • • • • • • • • • • • •

Heinemann Library
Chicago, Illinois

© 2000 Reed Educational & Professional Publishing
Published by Heinemann Library,
an imprint of Reed Educational & Professional Publishing,
100 North LaSalle, Suite 1010
Chicago, IL 60602

Customer Service 1-888-454-2279

Designed by Celia Floyd
Originated by HBM Print Ltd, Singapore
Printed in Hong Kong by Wing King Tong

04 03 02 01 00
10 9 8 7 6 5 4 3 2 1

Library of Congress Cataloging-in-Publication Data
Bizley, Kirk.
   Mountain biking / Kirk Bizley.
        p. cm. -- (Radical sports)
   Includes bibliographical references (p.) and index.
   Summary: A beginner's guide to mountain biking, with a brief
history of the sport and tips on choosing equipment, finding places
to bike, and performing basic maneuvers.
   ISBN 1-57572-944-X (lb)
   1. All terrain cycling Juvenile literature. [1. All terrain
cycling.] I. Title. II. Series.
GV1056.B59 1999
796.6'3--DC21   99-24038
                                                  CIP

Acknowledgments
The Publishers would like to thank the following for permission to reproduce photographs:

Mary Evans Picture Library, p. 4; Chris Honeywell, pp. 10-11, 13, 15; Stockfile/Steven Behr, pp. 6, 8, 9, 12, 16-28; Stockfile/Malcolm Fearon, pp. 5 bottom, 29 bottom; Stockfile/Jim McRoy, p. 29 top.

Cover photograph reproduced with permission of Action Plus/Neal Haynes

Our thanks to Patrice Quintero of the National Off-Road Bicycle Association for her valuable comments in the preparation of this book.

Some words in this book are in bold, **like this**. You can find out what they mean by looking in the Glossary.

CONTENTS

Introduction 4

What Is a Mountain Bike? 6

The Bike for You...............................8

What Else Do You Need?.................10

Keeping Fit and Healthy.................12

Before You Start.............................14

Biking Skills

    Town Biking 16

    Off-road Skills 18

    Dealing with Obstacles............20

    Dealing with Different Terrains.....22

Taking it Further.............................24

Essential Maintenance.....................26

The International Scene 28

Glossary 30

Useful Addresses 31

More Books to Read.......................31

Index...32

INTRODUCTION

The first bicycle, made in France in the 1690s, was just a wooden beam with wheels attached to it. The cyclist would sit on a cushion and steer with his feet. Biking has certainly come a long way since then!

Important developments

Since the 17th century, there have been considerable changes. Here are some of the important advances and the dates when they were made:

1791	An early type of bike known as the **celerifere** was exhibited at the Palais Royale in Paris. It was a wooden beam with wheels.
1816	The first two-wheeled bike with steering was made in Germany. In England, they were known as **hobby horses**. Two years later a slightly better version, called the **dandy horse**, was developed.
1839	A Scottish blacksmith named Kirkpatrick Macmillan added the first driving levers and pedals.
1855	The **velocipede** was made in France. It had a wooden frame and wheels; iron tires were attached to the front wheel.
1869	Solid rubber tires were added and the name "bicycle" was used for the first time.
1880	The first bike was produced with front and rear wheels of the same size, pedals with **sprockets**, and **gears** and chains. It also used ball bearings for smooth running and pneumatic (inflated) tires for a more comfortable ride.

These early bikes had no pedals or brakes and were just pushed along with the feet.

4

Cheap and efficient!

After cars became popular, fewer people used bikes to get around. But a renewed interest in cycling began in the 1960s and 70s, as people realized that cycling was a cheap, efficient, and environmentally friendly way of getting around!

In 1977, the first basic **all-terrain bikes (ATBs)** were developed in the United States. They had reinforced frames, chunky tires for improved grip, and racing-bike gears.

In 1980, an American company named Specialized put out the first mass-produced mountain bike. At the same time, Japanese companies, such as Suntour, were making the first special components for mountain bikes.

This early Specialized Stump Jumper™ shows the strong frame and chunky tires that make a mountain bike.

Since 1980, progress and developments have been very rapid. Mountain bike cross-country racing became an Olympic event at the Atlanta Games in 1996.

5

WHAT IS A MOUNTAIN BIKE?

Tough, chunky, rugged, and durable are all words that describe the modern mountain bike. A mountain bike is designed for strength, versatility, and speed. It is ideal for hard workouts on tough terrain, which is why it is often referred to as an **all-terrain bike**.

Saddle and seat post

Some mountain bikes have seats with quick releases to allow for easy adjustment. To find the right setting, push one pedal down as low as it will go, so that the **pedal cranks** are vertical. If you are seated with the ball of your foot in the lowest pedal, your leg should be just slightly bent. The latest **suspension systems** on saddles make riding more comfortable.

Transmission and gearing system

The transmission includes the pedals, pedal crank set, chain, and the cogs on the rear wheel. These parts convert the power from your pedaling legs into the movement of the bike's rear wheel.

Most mountain bikes have 15 to 27 **gears**. The gearing system consists of the front and rear **derailleurs,** the rear **sprockets**, and the gear levers. The rider chooses the most appropriate gear for the terrain using the gear shifters on the handlebars. A wide choice of gears makes cycling easier, both uphill and downhill.

Frame

The frame is usually made from aluminum or an **alloy**, such as steel. These metals are strong yet relatively light. Recently, different materials such as titanium and carbon fiber have been used. These reduce the weight of the bike even more, making the bikes easier to maneuver and pedal uphill. In recent years, some models have also added front and rear suspension.

Steering system

This comprises the front fork, handlebars, handlebar stem, and the bearings of the headset. A strong and durable system gives you better steering precision. Extensions are available that bolt onto the ends of your handlebars to allow for extra riding positions.

Brakes

There are front and rear brakes which, when well-adjusted, allow you to slow down with fingertip control. **Cantilever brakes** (also called V brakes) are the most common type.

Wheels

Modern wheels are both light and strong. They are made with narrow aluminum rims that are light and very flexible. Chunky tires with good grips are fitted back and front, often with quick-release **hubs**. You can also get carbon rims that are even lighter and stronger, but also more expensive!

THE BIKE FOR YOU

Mountain bikes come in all shapes and sizes, but don't be confused. With planning and a little research, you will have no trouble finding the right bike for you.

Requirements

What sort of riding do you plan to do? If you are a beginner, then an all-purpose bike would be best. If you are going to try a lot of off-road riding or even racing, then you will need a specialty bike. Most manufacturers make special children's bikes and these can be fully adjusted—you can even get small adults' bikes. One of these types would probably be the best to start with.

Cost

You can pay over $2,000 for a top-of-the-line bike! When budgeting, don't forget to include the cost of a helmet, lock, lights, and other essential equipment, such as a water bottle carrier or flat tire repair kit.

Size

Your bike must be the right size for you. Bikes have different frame sizes and different wheel sizes. One simple test is to stand astride the bike with your feet flat on the floor and lift the bike off the ground. If the bike size is correct, there should be a gap of about two inches (five centimeters) between your tires and the ground.

You must get the right size bike frame. You can adjust the height to fit.

At the bike store

Compare all of the prices of the bikes on sale and make sure they have all the features you want, such as the right number of **gears** and type of tires.

Always have a test ride so that you can check that the size is right, that the bike feels comfortable, and that the brakes work properly. A salesperson can adjust the bike for you. You should always ask for a free first service, so that you can take the bike back for a check-up after you have ridden it.

A bike shop is usually the best place to buy a bike. The wide variety of bikes can be confusing, but the salespeople can answer any questions you might have.

SAFETY FIRST

Before buying a bike, make sure it is legal and **roadworthy**. Check especially that a second-hand bike has reasonable treads on the tires and the brakes work properly.

WHAT ELSE DO YOU NEED?

Before you go out on your mountain bike you should think carefully about what you need to wear and what you need to take with you. There is nothing wrong with wearing your own normal clothing. However, avoid anything loose-fitting that could get caught in the wheels or chain. For real comfort and added safety the right gear is essential.

Helmet

This is the most important piece of equipment. It can save your life! Make sure you get one that fits properly. It should fit low on your head (but not obstruct your vision) and snugly so that it does not wobble from side to side. Get the best quality helmet you can afford—the investment is well worth it! Try a few on and ask an expert for advice. This girl is wearing a special downhilling helmet with chin protection, but a regular bike helmet will be enough for all but the roughest courses.

Arms and upper body

You should wear a long-sleeved shirt made of moisture-wicking material. It is also a good idea to wear elbow pads for rough courses.

Gloves

You should wear gloves. Padded cycling mitts are not enough—you really need some tough full-fingered gloves that will give you full protection.

Cycling shorts

You can buy padded lycra cycling shorts (much more comfortable on that hard saddle!) and as long as you wear them without underwear and wash them after every trip they are the best way to avoid any soreness.

PROTECTION FROM PAIN

You need to protect any parts of your body that you can—you will be riding over rough territory and falling off can be painful!

Sunglasses

For perfect vision and complete eye protection you should buy a good pair of sunglasses with lenses that can be changed depending on the weather conditions.

Legs

For rough terrain, a sturdy pair of jeans will protect your legs, but cycling tights allow more movement. If you are going to be downhilling, you might like to add some knee pads for extra protection!

Shoes

You can wear just ordinary sneakers, but you can also buy special pedal/shoe combinations that have a stiff shoe sole with a cleat system—a system that easily attaches and detaches your shoe from the pedal.

KEEPING FIT AND HEALTHY

Riding a bike on rough terrain can be quite hard work. You will need to have a good level of general fitness. Cycling itself is one of the best ways to get fit!

Warm-up

Before each riding session you should do a **warm-up** to get your body properly prepared for what is to come. It's a good idea to stretch out the parts of your body that you will be using—this can prevent injuries. It will also keep you from being sore the next day! All of these exercises are just examples.

Cool-down

When you ride your bike, you are in a fairly fixed position, and you might find that you are very stiff when you get off. This is why you should do a cool-down when you finish. You can repeat your warm-up routine, but not for so long. This gives your body a chance to recover.

Neck stretch ······

Gently pull your head towards your shoulders. Hold for 10 seconds, then do the other side.

Quadricep stretch

Bend one knee and pull your foot up behind you. Hold this for 10 seconds, then do the other leg. ··········

····· *Hamstring stretch*

Sit as shown and reach for your toes, keeping your head down. Hold for 10 seconds. Repeat six times for each leg.

Lower back stretch·

Lying on your back, bend one knee up to your chest and lift your head and shoulders to meet it. Lower yourself. Do this six times before doing the other side.

The right food

If you are going to be doing a lot of riding, make sure that you are eating the right foods. If you plan to go riding for over an hour, take some food along to eat, as well as plenty of water.

These are good choices for mountain bikers:

- Bananas are high in ....➤ **carbohydrates**, which give energy.

- Dried fruit also makes a good.................... high-energy snack.

- Energy bars come in many .... flavors and are good for quick bursts of energy.

- Water or a sports drink will help prevent **dehydration.**

The main advantage of all of these foods is that they are light and easy to carry. You can attach a water bottle to the frame of your bike so that you can take drinks as you are riding. Try to drink at least a bottle of water every hour, more in hot weather.

BEFORE YOU START

Mountain biking is a dangerous sport and can lead to injury. There is a chance that you could have a bad crash and be lying injured in a very inaccessible spot. You should never ride alone in a remote area.

Prepare for the worst

If you do decide to go by yourself on an off-road ride, make sure that you tell someone responsible where you are going and how long you expect to be gone. That way, if you have an accident, someone will know where you are and can get help to you.

Pre-ride checks

Before you go off on your bike, you should always perform these safety checks:

- Make sure that you have enough time to complete your planned route in daylight—you don't want to be off-road in the dark!
- Check the weather forecast. Severe weather can also cause you problems, especially in hilly areas.

BE SEEN!

🚲 Your bike must have front and rear reflectors. You should also add lights for safety. Even in sunlight, it is a good idea to wear bright clothing so drivers can see you.

Before you start, make sure that you are wearing the correct safety equipment and that your bike is in a **roadworthy** condition.

What to pack

In addition to your food, there are some other items you should take:

- plenty of water to drink, so that there is no danger of becoming **dehydrated**.

- basic spares and tools for your bike, such as a flat tire repair kit.

- sunscreen—it is very easy to get sunburned on a bike, even in cloudy weather.

- insect repellent—nothing will ruin a ride faster than bug bites!

- money—you should take enough for a ride home if you have trouble with your bike, and at least enough for an emergency telephone call.

Flat tire repair kit

Sunscreen

Insect repellent

SAFETY FIRST

Remember to put on all the necessary protective clothing. Don't forget that helmet—it could save your life!

15

TOWN BIKING

Checklist

The first place you are likely to ride your bike is around town. There are a few things you should check before you do this.

1. Are you confident on your bike, well-balanced on the saddle, and unlikely to fall over? Is your balance good enough for you to be able to look from side to side with confidence?

2. Do you know the rules of the road? If not, then you need to learn. Bicycles are required to follow the same traffic rules as cars. You can join a local club that will teach you all the basics, such as the correct hand signals.

Steering

Steering is an essential skill. At low speeds, you must turn your handlebars to steer. As you turn the corner, the bike will lean, so allow your body to lean with it. For **high-speed turns** the bike will lean with you naturally and take you around a corner—you will only have to use the handlebars a little.

You will need to be able to lean your bike into corners as you go around them.

Gear changing

Your mountain bike will have a lot of **gears**, and you need to get used to selecting the right gears and changing them. The lower the gear, the easier it is to pedal, so you need a low gear to go uphill and a high gear for flat areas and downhill. Try to ride in the gear that is most comfortable for you.

You should always try to change gears when you are not pushing too hard on the pedals, so ease off before each gear change. Try out all of the gears on your bike and practice changing from one to another until you can do it smoothly and safely.

You should not have to strain too hard or stand up in the saddle—when it is hard work, change down a gear.

Braking

You have both a front and rear brake on your bike, so make sure you know which is which! If you pull on your front brake too quickly you may flip forward over the handlebars, or the front tire may lose its grip. Always try to slow down by applying the rear brake first, then lightly squeezing the front one.

You should not go on to any other form of riding until you have mastered all of these basic skills!

Remember, you don't have to put your brakes fully on or fully off—you can gently apply your brakes just to slow down.

SAFETY FIRST

🚲 Always try to slow down gradually and avoid **emergency braking**.

OFF-ROAD SKILLS

You have learned that you must move your body weight to stay in balance while turning corners. This technique is equally important when learning the following skills.

Going downhill

Descending is one of the most exciting parts of riding your mountain bike. However, you will be traveling at higher speeds and the chances of an accident are greater, so be careful!

Keep your weight back as far over the rear wheel as you can and start to apply your brakes slowly (this is known as **feathering**). You might need to stand up slightly on the pedals so that your legs act like a **suspension system** and absorb shocks. Keep feathering your brakes but keep your hands wide on the handlebars to get maximum control.

Going downhill in areas such as this requires practice and skillful riding.

SAFETY FIRST

Start off with a gentle slope and make sure you can cope with that before you go on to really steep ones!

Going uphill

Climbing, or **ascending**, can be very hard work, and you will be glad of all the **gears** you have on your mountain bike.

Before you start climbing a hill or slope, make sure that you have selected the right gear. It is easier to change gears before you get to the really steep part. Try to keep your weight forward and quite low. Stay sitting in the saddle. This way you get a better grip, or **traction**, and it will give you more power to get up the hill. For extreme climbs, you may need to stand out of the saddle.

Remember to keep looking ahead of you to find the easiest route up and avoid any obstacles that might be in your way!

Cornering

You will corner much slower than usual if you are going uphill and much faster if you are going downhill, so you have to know what to do!

The basic rule of cornering is that you should always brake before you are at the corner. You must also lean into the corner while extending your outside leg to balance your weight.

You might have to do a **low-speed turn** if you are ascending and you should be able to make it tight. If you are descending on a **high-speed turn** you need to make as wide a turn as you can.

SAFETY FIRST

You never know what might be around a tight corner—another rider, or perhaps a walker. So always be ready to brake and stop if necessary.

DEALING WITH OBSTACLES

If you practice your front wheel lift, you will not only be able to lift your bike over curbs, but you can also do wheelies!

When you are off-road you will come across many obstacles. One of the best things about having your mountain bike is that once you learn the right techniques, you can go right over them!

Front wheel lift
The most basic technique is the **front wheel lift**, which you can use to get up and over curbs or logs.

Keep the bike in a low **gear**, slide your weight back, and bend down, keeping your elbows low. Push down with your strongest leg with its pedal high and then lift the handlebars up at the same time, moving your weight back. This should lift the front wheel up off the ground.

SAFETY FIRST

🚲 Remember to wear all the proper safety equipment at all times, especially your helmet!

🚲 Never ride over an edge or slope without knowing the height of the drop first!

Bunny hop
There may be times when you and your bike have to take off completely. This maneuver is known as a bunny hop. This is not as difficult as it looks—and it is great fun!

Try it on some level, soft grass at first. Pedal along and decide where you want to jump. Before you get there, bend down over the bike with your weight low. When you want to jump, spring your body up and lift up the handlebars at the same time. As soon as the front wheel starts to lift, pull up your legs and feet so that the rear wheel lifts as well. Don't forget that you will be coming down as well! Relax your arms and legs and allow them to absorb the shock of your landing. Try to level the bike out so that both wheels land at the same time.

Doing jumps on your bike can be fun but requires a lot of practice.

Dropping off

You might find that you get airborne quite often, especially if you are riding fast towards steep edges or slopes. Going over these in the air is known as "dropping off." Keep your pedals level, lift the front wheel off as you go over the edge, and then use the same techniques for the landing as you did with your bunny hop. You might be coming down from a bit of a height, so make sure you really relax your arms and legs as you land!

Dropping off can be dangerous. Never do it unless you have checked the area first.

DEALING WITH DIFFERENT TERRAINS

One of the best things about mountain biking is being able to go over different types of terrain that would be too rough for a street bike. Each type will require slightly different skills.

Mud

You can just about guarantee that you will have to ride through mud. Wherever possible, try to go around particularly muddy areas, because you can get stuck in thick mud.

Leaning back and lifting the front wheel allows the back wheel to grip and helps you cycle through muddy areas.

As you approach a muddy area, make sure that you are in a low **gear** and keep your weight back in the saddle and towards the rear of the bike. Try to keep pedaling right through the mud—if you stop you are likely to get stuck. The drive force is coming from your rear wheel, so try to keep the front wheel up and your weight back until you come out of the mud. You can then transfer your weight forward to put the front wheel down onto firmer ground.

Water

You may come across a puddle or even a stream or river. Always make sure that you do not enter water that is too deep—if it comes up above the level of the center **hub** of your wheels, you should not ride into it.

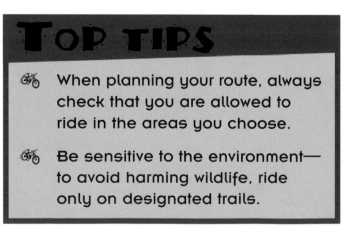

TOP TIPS

🚴 When planning your route, always check that you are allowed to ride in the areas you choose.

🚴 Be sensitive to the environment— to avoid harming wildlife, ride only on designated trails.

When you ride through water, make sure that you are in a low gear, and reduce your speed. Go into the water slowly, lifting your front wheel slightly, and continue to pedal. Increase your speed as you come out of the water, but be careful, because your tires will be wet and slippery. Also remember that your wheel rims will be wet—this will reduce the efficiency of your brakes!

🚲 Never enter water if you are not sure how deep it is!

Always check your brakes after riding through water. Testing them helps to dry them off.

Gravel and sand

These materials are loose and difficult to ride through. Sand can be very tiring because it is so difficult to get a good grip on it. Use a low gear in these conditions and grip your handlebars tightly so that you are not thrown off track. You also have to be careful of stones or chips flying up towards you or other riders. Always keep your distance from other cyclists as they pass through gravel or you may be hit by grit flying up from their rear tires!

Hold tight and be careful when riding through loose, rough materials—they will make your steering wobble.

TAKING IT FURTHER

Now that you have learned the basic skills of mountain biking, you may want to take it further. If you want to ride more seriously or competitively, there are many local clubs that organize the following events.

Cross-country

These events usually take place on a loop track, from less than a mile to 6 miles (1 to 10 kilometers) long. Usually everyone starts together, with the fastest riders at the front. The course often involves hills, flat runs, and descents. The fastest rider usually wins!

Crossing water is part of the challenge of a cross-country race.

Cyclocross

Cyclocross is rapidly gaining popularity in the U.S. Because it is competed in winter, many bikers use it to stay in shape during the off-season.

A cyclocross course is usually about 3 miles (5 kilometers) long. The course includes paved road, dirt, sand pits, mud puddles, streams, and even fences! Bikers must dismount and carry their bikes over or around some obstacles. There are pit stops every few laps to fix bikes if necessary. Many cyclocross riders use modified road bikes, but mountain bikes can be used as well.

Downhill

This is becoming more and more popular. It is a type of **time trial**, which means that each rider rides down the course once, alone, and the fastest time is the winner! It involves rough terrain, so you must wear the correct protective equipment, including a helmet with chin protection.

Dual slalom

This is like a **downhill** event, except two riders ride down a course at the same time, swerving in and out and around poles, often making jumps as well! This is usually a thrilling competition, especially the final, which features the two best riders!

Downhill is a timed event and you have to finish the course as quickly as possible.

These two cyclists are competing against each other in this dual slalom.

If you want your bike to perform properly and safely, you must take good care of it. If you have a major problem with it, you will need to take it to a shop or dealer to get it fixed, but there are quite a few things you can do yourself, to prevent larger problems.

General checks

Before you go out on your bike you should spend a few minutes checking its basic components. If you do find a problem, get it fixed! Nothing is worse than being far from home and having to walk back because you did not check something properly. You should get a **manual** when you buy your bike. This will give you full details on what to check and what you can adjust yourself.

Brakes

The **brake blocks** or pads will wear down because they are designed to rub against the rim of the wheel. Check that they are in the right position (level with the wheels) and that they have not worn down too much. Adjusting them and replacing them is very easy, and only takes a couple of minutes—time very well spent!

You should also regularly check the brake cables for any sign of damage, especially fraying. Some bikes have a **cable adjuster** on the brake levers. If the brake cables are getting loose with wear, you can use the cable adjusters to tighten them.

Wheels and tires

Your tires are in contact with the ground all the time you are riding, so they are bound to get worn. The most annoying thing to get is a flat tire, so check for wear and look out for any thorns or pieces of glass or wire on your tires. Keep your tires pumped up—you are much less likely to get a flat if your tires are fully inflated. Also, make sure that the tread has not worn down. If it has, it is time to get a new tire!

Cleaning and oiling

Your bike is going to get dirty if you are riding off-road, and you will need to clean it when you get home. Wash it with warm, soapy water to get most of the mud and dirt off, then oil or grease the moving parts. Your manual will tell you how.

The chainset, **gears**, and pedals need **lubricating** regularly. They may also need some minor adjustments, such as tightening up nuts and bolts. These are some of the more complicated parts of your bike, so you may want to ask an expert to show you how.

You should be prepared to replace some parts of your bike that will wear out. If you check them carefully and regularly, especially before riding and when you get back, you can avoid breakdowns when you are out riding.

SAFETY FIRST

If you have any doubts about the safety or maintenance of your bike, take it to a specialist shop or mechanic to be thoroughly checked.

Mountain biking is quite a new sport. The first competitive races were in Marin County, California, in the 1980s.

The first championships

The first World Mountain Biking Championships were held in Durango, Colorado, in 1990. The first mountain biking World Cup Series took place in 1991, with entrants from Europe and North America. At that time, cross-country racing was the only event. It was not until 1993 that a six-event **downhill** World Cup was added.

World Cup Series

The World Cup Series involves riders from all over the world and takes place over about eight months in different countries.

The events can be on any type of course, from alpine mountains to city parks, and each race lasts from about one and a half to two hours.

One of the most successful early riders was Henrik Djernis from Denmark, who won the World Championship in 1994 for the third time in a row!

Downhill events

These are some of the most popular international events, and they are especially popular with the television networks. There is usually a limit of about 140 riders for the actual race. If more enter, there are qualifying events to select the fastest 90. They go into the semifinals against the top 50 riders in the world standings. These races are becoming more and more difficult and dangerous, and riders now wear full **body armor** and **full-face helmets**.

World Championships

The most important event of the year is the World Mountain Bike Championships—this is the one that all riders want to win. It is held every year in a different country, and it takes place over five days.

The course is selected very carefully and includes long sections of technical single track, a climb at altitude, technical fast downhills, and a variety of different surfaces. The riders who take part in these types of events are usually professionals. They take training and racing very seriously.

Shaun Palmer competes in the downhill race of the 1997 World Championships.

Downhill events are competed over very challenging courses and at great speeds.

GLOSSARY

alloy metal that is mixed with one or more other elements

all-terrain bike (ATB) another term for a mountain bike

ascending going uphill

body armor protective clothing worn by downhill racers

brake block part of the brake that is in contact with the wheel rim

cable adjuster brake adjuster found in the brake levers

cantilever brake brake that moves on a pivot in order to exert pressure on either side of a wheel's rim

carbohydrate nutrient that the body needs to supply it with energy

celerifere early type of bike made in France

dandy horse early type of bike

dehydration when the body lacks or has a shortage of fluids such as water

derailleur bicycle part that works by changing the line of the chain to a different sprocket while pedaling

descending going downhill

downhill specific competitive event where riders race on a downhill course

emergency braking pulling on the brakes very hard and quickly

feathering gently pulling the brake on and off to control speed

front wheel lift technique where you lift the front wheel up off the ground over an obstacle

full-face helmet safety helmet that covers the whole face and head of a rider

gears mechanism of moving parts that can transmit or regulate motion

high-speed turn cornering very fast, usually on a downhill course

hobby horse first type of bike that had steering

hub central part of a wheel

low-speed turn cornering at low speed, usually when on an uphill course

lubricating greasing or oiling various parts of your bike as necessary

manual instruction booklet that usually comes with a new bike and gives detailed information about it

pedal crank arm that joins a pedal to the bottom bracket on a bike

roadworthy in good condition overall and suitable to ride

sprocket cog on a bike, such as those driven by the chain

suspension system spring and shock absorbers used to absorb jolting and protect the bike from damage

time trial road race in which the winner is the rider with the fastest time

traction amount of grip a tire has on the ground

velocipede early type of bike with iron tires

warm-up series of stretching exercises you should perform before riding to prepare your body

USEFUL ADDRESSES

Mountain biking has become so popular that you can find local clubs almost anywhere. Your local bike shop is a good place to find out about clubs and competitions. Here are addresses for some of the national and international cycling organizations. They run most of the larger competitions and are good sources of information on cycling events.

International Mountain Bicycling
Association (IMBA)
P.O. Box 7578
Boulder, CO 80306
303-545-9011

National Off-Road Bicycle Association
(NORBA)
Building 6, One Olympic Plaza
Colorado Springs, CO 80909
719-578-4581

Union Cycliste Internationale (UCI)
International Cycling Union
37 Route de Chavannes
Case Postale
CH 1000 Lausanne 23
Switzerland

MORE BOOKS TO READ

Armentrout, David. *Mountain Biking.* Vero Beach, Fla.: Rourke Book Company, Inc. 1997.

Brimner, Larry D. *Mountain Biking.* Danbury, Conn.: Franklin Watts, Inc., 1997.

Evans, Jeremy. *Off-Road Biking.* Parsippany, N.J.: Silver Burdett Press, 1992.

Hautzig, David. *Pedal Power: How a Mountain Bike Is Made.* N.Y.: Dutton Children's Books, 1996.

King, Andy. *Fundamental Mountain Biking.* Minneapolis: The Lerner Publishing Group, 1996.

Richards, Brant. *Fantastic Book of Mountain Biking.* Brookfield, Conn.: Millbrook Press, Incorporated, 1998.

Seidl, Herman. *Mountain Bikes: Maintaining, Repairing, & Upgrading.* N.Y.: Sterling Publishing Company, Inc., 1992.

INDEX

accessories   10–11

all-terrain bikes   5, 6

brake blocks   26

brakes   7, 9, 17, 26

bunny hop   20–21

cable adjuster   26

cantilever brakes   7

cool-down   12

cornering   19

cross-country racing   5, 24

cycling shorts   10

cyclocross   24

derailleur   6

different terrains   22–23

downhill   25, 28–29

dropping off   21

dual slalom   25

early bikes   4, 5

elbow pads   10

emergency braking   17

feathering   18

frame   7, 8

front wheel lift   20

gear changing   17

gears   4, 6, 9, 17, 19, 20, 22, 23, 27

gloves   10

health and fitness   12–13

helmet   10

knee pads   11

low-speed turn   19

maintenance   26–27

nutrition   13

off-road biking   18–19, 20–21

Olympics   5

pedal crank   6

pre-ride checks   14–15, 16

puncture repair kit   8, 15

reflectors   14

safety checks   14

shoes   11

sprockets   4, 6

steering system   7

stretches   12

Stump Jumper™   5

sunglasses   11

suspension system   6, 18

time trial   25

town biking   16–17

transmission   6

turning   16–17

warm-up   12

weather   14

wheels   7, 10, 27

World Championships   29

World Cup series   28